How to Make rubbings

How to

Make rubbings

Michael Kingsley Skinner

STUDIO VISTA London

VAN NOSTRAND REINHOLD COMPANY New York

Acknowledgments
The author would like to thank the Vicar of the parish of Walton-on-Thames for giving him permission to rub brasses in his church; his sister Elizabeth for typing the MS; and everyone else who gave help or encouragement. The colour photographs are by Peter Hirst-Smith.

A Studio Vista/Van Nostrand Reinhold How-to Book

Photoset by BAS Printers Limited, Wallop, Hampshire
Printed in Great Britain

Published in Great Britain by
Studio Vista
Blue Star House, Highgate Hill, London N19
and in the United States by
Van Nostrand Reinhold Company
A Division of Litton Educational Publishing, Inc.
450 West 33rd Street, New York, N.Y. 10001.

Library of Congress Catalog Card Number 75-161977
ISBN 0 289 70190 2

Contents

Introduction

This book has been designed primarily for children, but I hope that other members of the family will find in it much to interest them as well.

My aim has been to show how much pleasure and fun may be derived from this 'art form', and at the same time to make readers more aware of the textures and shapes of things around them.

The variety of materials and the variations in which this craft may be applied are endless and allow full scope to the imagination. The method is simple, execution speedy, and results give immediate satisfaction.

M.K.S.

How to make a simple rubbing

A rubbing is an easy way to make a copy of a surface of an object.

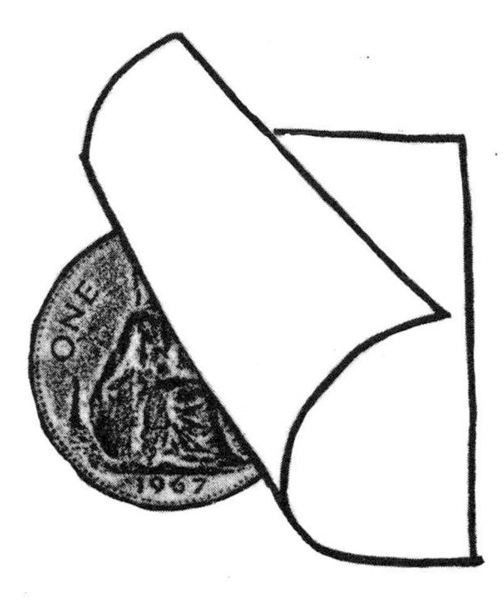

Place an object – a coin, perhaps – under a piece of paper. Then, with a pencil or crayon, 'rub' the surface of the coin through the paper. You will see your copy appearing immediately.

Many ancient, foreign and modern coins, medals and badges have interesting designs.

You could make a collection of kings and queens, for example, or of animals.

Before you start rubbing, fix the underside of each object to the table with adhesive tape.

Cut out your best rubbings and stick them in a note-book, arranging them rather like a stamp collection.

UNITED STATES OF AMERICA
HALF DOLLAR
ONE PENNY
1967
VICTORIA REGINA
1956
L.50
FID DEF
SIXPENCE
NEW PENCE
2
THE AFRICA STAR
VI

Try rubbing other things using black wax crayon and white paper, not too thick. Hold the paper firmly while you are rubbing so as not to spoil the pattern.

There are many things in the house and garden that make good rubbings. Here are just a few ideas: wood, sandpaper, raised wall-paper, lace, cut glass, book bindings, fossils, string, chain.

Experimenting with different materials

Rubbing on aluminium foil

Ordinary kitchen foil will probably prove too thin for some rubbings. Thicker foil may be bought from shops selling artists' materials, and milkbottle tops and disposable metal dishes are ideal for small rubbings.

Lay the foil on the object you wish to rub and fix it in position with masking tape. Work over the area with a nailbrush to press the foil into the pattern underneath. *Never* use foil when rubbing a brass.

If you make a rubbing of a surface or out of doors, wrap the foil round a cardboard tube to avoid creasing it on the way home.

Strengthening and mounting a foil rubbing

Lay the foil face down on a flat surface and cover it with several coats of fibreglass resin or sodium silicate (waterglass). Allow each coat to harden before applying the next.

When it is completely dry, turn the foil over and fill in the lines or grooves by lightly rubbing in liquid shoe black or lino printing ink, Indian ink, or similar.

When it is dry, clean off any surplus ink by working over the flat areas with fine steel wool.

Your rubbing can now be left as it is or cut out carefully and stuck with quick-drying glue onto dark-coloured cardboard or hardboard. It will also look very effective glued to a door. Be careful not to leave any lumps of glue on the back of the rubbing.

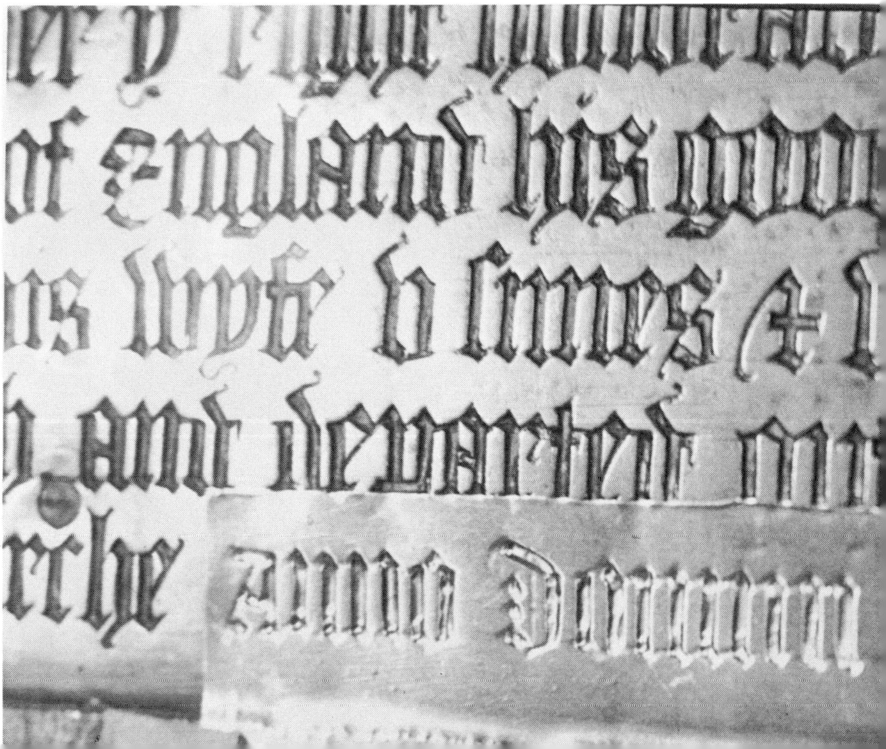

right honorable
ngland his good
departed out of this
of englannd his
and departed
Anno

Using white wax
Instead of using dark wax on white paper, why not try white wax on a dark paper.

You could even go one step further and use white wax on a white paper. This will give a quite different result, and is known as 'resist' method.

Rub the wax over the object in the usual way, making sure the paper is held firmly. Now take a large, soft brush and, using ink or water colour paints, paint over the design lightly. Keep the brush moving in the same direction all the time. At once you will see the design appearing.

Using different coloured waxes
It is possible to buy special non-smudge wax crayons in a variety of bright colours (see page 66).

Try using more than one colour for the same rubbing. Make a rubbing of a leaf with one side one colour and the other side another.

When you have finished the rubbing, polish it with a clean cloth. This will give it a shiny surface.

Various shades of metallic sticks are available from art and craft shops (page 66). These will produce interesting effects when used singly or together – particularly the gold and bronze.

In most cases a dark colour paper is particularly effective as a background.

Making patterns and designs

Leaves

You can make interesting patterns and decorative pictures from leaves. There are hundreds of shapes and sizes from which to choose.

Arrange them first on a piece of paper or card, then stick them down with a quick-drying glue. Lay a sheet of paper on top and then rub, lightly at first, keeping the crayon working in the same direction all the time.

You may like to cut some leaves in half to help the design, or perhaps cut a hole in a leaf to represent an animal's eye.

Odds and ends

See how many different fairly flat objects you can find, such as keys, paper clips, parts of an old clock or toy, safety pins, curtain rings and hooks, chain, washers, matches, string, staples and combs.

Now try arranging them into patterns or decorative animals. Cut a piece of cardboard the size of the design you like best. Cover the card with glue and lay the objects on it one by one. Leave to dry. Now lay a sheet of paper over the design and fix it to the cardboard with adhesive tape before you begin rubbing.

You may prefer to glue only one part of the card at a time, especially if the design is large. Try spreading the glue with a scrap of old thick card. You will find this better than a brush which is difficult to clean if the glue hardens on it.

You can mix several different objects together in your design or use just one kind on their own. Why not try a design in string like the one on page 25? You may find it necessary to pin the string to the cardboard with drawing pins until the glue is dry.

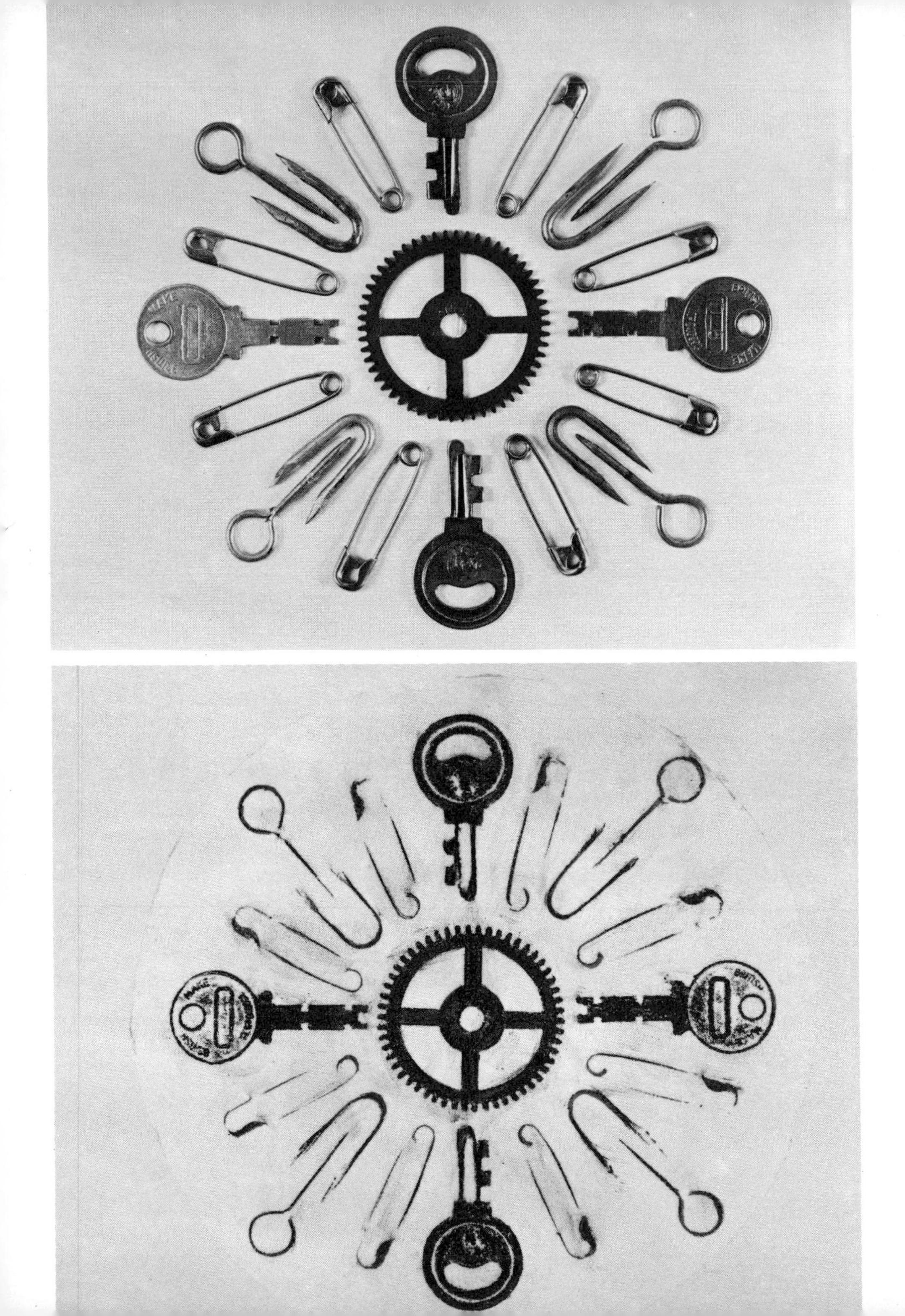

Your name or initials

You need: wax crayon, pencil, paper, cardboard,
scissors, cutting knife and glue

Draw the letters of your name or initials onto the piece of cardboard. If you prefer, you can use the letters printed on an empty food or detergent packet. Whichever you choose, make sure that the card is thicker than the paper you intend to use.

Cut out the letters and try arranging them in different ways, putting some on top of each other. Glue the design you like best onto a piece of cardboard.

Lay a sheet of paper over the top, hold it down firmly, and rub it with crayon.

You can rub the same design over and over again. If it is small enough, you could use it to mark your books or make your own headed notepaper.

TEXTURE
FISH

Dabbing

This method can be used when the engraving on the object has such shallow lines that the wax crayon does not give sufficient detail.

First make a dabber by wrapping a square of chamois leather lightly round a ball of cotton wool and tying it in place.

Mix some powdered graphite or powdered pencil lead with a few drops of linseed or olive oil to make a paste. Do the mixing on a piece of board, thick card or hardboard.

Cover the object with a sheet of tissue paper or other thin paper and hold it in place with masking tape. Now dab some of the graphite mixture onto the paper with your dabber. Try to get an even finish and avoid any rubbing movement as this will move the paper.

This method can take a considerable time if a large area has to be covered. The result will not be as black as a wax rubbing.

Your dabbing should now be 'fixed' with a special fixative to prevent smudging. This can be bought from most good shops selling artists' materials.

Brass rubbing

'Monumental brasses' or, simply, 'brasses' are to be found in many old churches. They are made of flat sheets of brass which have been engraved with figures, coats of arms, and sometimes inscriptions. They are set into a stone slab on the floor or wall of the church. Some of them are over six hundred years old.

Perhaps you will find one in your local church or in other churches when you are away on holiday.

Materials

You need: heelball – a mixture of wax and lamp-black, obtainable from most shoe repairers

or: Astral sticks – these are specially made for brass rubbing and do not smudge. They may be bought from the suppliers listed on page 66.

paper – lining paper, white or coloured papers may be used, provided they are not too thick. Architects' detail white paper is the best and it will not turn yellow with age. Never use metal foil on brasses.

masking tape (*not* ordinary adhesive tape)

scissors

a clean cloth

Permission to rub must be obtained in advance from the vicar or rector of the church. This can save disappointment, as you may arrive and find that someone else is rubbing. You will find that some churches do not allow rubbing on Sundays. A fee is usually charged.

How to make a brass rubbing

1 Clean the brass very carefully with your cloth to remove grit or dust which could scratch the brass or tear your paper.

2 Lay the paper over the brass and hold it firmly in position with strips of masking tape.

3 With your finger and clean cloth, find the edge of the brass and press slightly to mark the outline. This will help to prevent rubbing over the edge.

4 Start rubbing at the top of the figure and work towards the feet. You must press hard with the heelball if you wish to obtain a dark, even effect. When rubbing the edge of the design, hold the paper down firmly with your hand.

5 When the rubbing is finished, dust away any loose flakes of heelball. Polish it with a clean cloth to make the wax shine. It is now ready to mount or display.

How to mount your rubbing

You need: strong glue
card
string or coloured cord
a length of rod, bamboo or dowelling

1 Cut two pieces of the rod a little wider than your paper.

2 Lay your rubbing out flat. Roll one end of the paper twice round a piece of rod. Fix it with strong glue. Do the same to the other end.

3 Knot the cord firmly to each end of the top rod.

You may prefer to cut round the edge of your rubbing, especially if you have rubbed over the edge of the outline by mistake. Paste it onto white or coloured paper or even onto a fabric such as hessian. Then mount it as described above.

Clear plastic polyester film, which will not stretch or shrink, may be placed over the rubbing as a substitute for glass. Fix it in position with masking tape on the back of your mounted rubbing.

The brass on the facing page was mounted on textured wallpaper.

Rubbing on tissue paper

White tissue paper has already been mentioned in the section on Dabbing (page 28), but coloured tissue papers can also be used to great effect. A wide range of colours is available from most large stores and stationers.

As the paper is very thin you should avoid rubbing objects with sharp raised edges. If you rub leaves, cut away any hard stalks before rubbing so as to reduce the chances of tearing the paper.

You can give your paper a pretty, mottled effect if you wish. Simply choose two or more coloured papers. Sprinkle them with cold water and lay one on top of the other. Allow them to dry before you separate them.

Remember to fix the underneath of the object to a firm surface with glue or adhesive tape before starting your rubbing. Lay tissue paper over the top and rub lightly.

Contrasting light coloured papers with a dark wax can look very effective, as shown on the facing page.

When finished the paper can be framed, mounted, or used as attractive wrapping paper for gifts.

Rubbing on fabric

A wide variety of materials are suitable for the making of rubbings – cotton, linen (old sheets or pillow cases), muslin, silk, broadcloth, and many others.

Naturally, the thicker the material you use, the more likely you are to lose some of the detail. It is essential to hold the material firmly in position over the object to be rubbed. Fabric is inclined to stretch, and may distort the design.

The more open or coarse materials give an interesting textured background to the rubbed design, but in this case also it will lose a certain amount of detail.

To 'fix' the crayon, lightly iron the reverse side of the material.

Your designs could be used as patterns for embroidery, or you could use the material for dressing puppets. The possibilities are endless.

Ideas for rubbings

Tombstones

You will find that in many old churches tombstones have been let into the floor or walls. Some have interesting crests, designs, or decorative writing and make very good rubbings. You need not rub the whole of a stone, but only the area you like best.

If you are rubbing out of doors, make sure your paper is securely taped down as it can easily blow away. Sometimes tape will not adhere to soft powdery stone and you will have to wrap the paper right round the stone so that you can tape the two ends of the paper together.

As in the case of brass rubbings, you should ask permission to rub. Usually no rubbing is allowed on Sundays. No fee is likely to be charged for this kind of rubbing.

Commemorative stones or foundation stones are often just as interesting as tombstones.

1799
1687.
Æt. 66.

Horse brasses

These objects make very good rubbings. It is thought that they were originally attached to horses' harness to ward off evil spirits or bad luck. There are hundreds of designs to be found. Some of the patterns are very old and are based on ancient superstitions; others are just decorative or commemorative. You will still see horses wearing them on Show days.

V R
1870

Furniture fittings

Most of these are made of brass or other metals and some can make good rubbings. Keys, keyhole covers, hinges, fingerplates and handles can all make unusual patterns and designs. Many interesting ones will be found on old doors and antique furniture.

Cast iron
There is a vast amount of cast iron adding decoration to our streets. It is easy to pass this ironwork without noticing it, yet once you have become aware of its presence you will keep seeing new items.

Some pieces, such as milestones or boundary stones, may be very old. Some may bear city crests.

You can make an interesting collection of these or use them as decoration like the manhole covers on page 56. Remember to fix your paper securely with masking tape before starting to rub and try to work the wax evenly.

The names, badges and number plates of the vehicles that use the roads have a particularly wide variety of designs.

USA I
B
H
35FT 9"
MANOR ROAD
NL
FH
11FTS
7223PJ
MG
GR

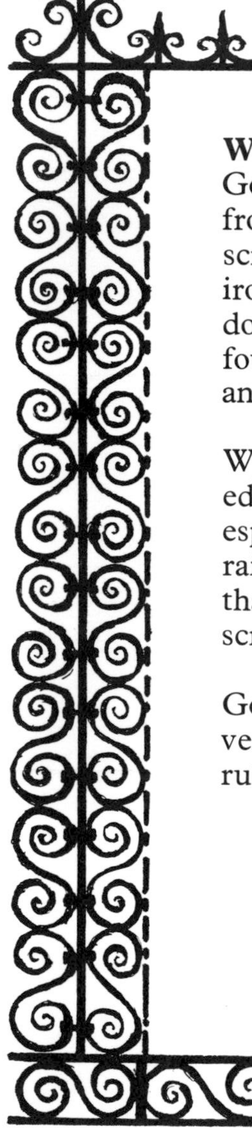

Wrought iron
Good rubbings can be made from the beautiful patterns of scrolls and motifs on wrought iron gates, screens, grilles and doors. They are mostly to be found in churches, cathedrals and ancient buildings.

Work carefully, feeling the edge of the design as you rub, especially when you come to raised areas such as a collar that has been used to strap the scrolls together.

Gold wax on black paper is very effective for this type of rubbing.

Watermarks

To rub a watermark you need paper, a soft drawing pencil, and a piece of glass or mirror to use as a working surface. Not all paper is suitable. Architects' detail paper is ideal as it is not too thick and has very little grain.

Lay the watermarked paper on the piece of glass. If you are going to rub a postage stamp, lay it face down. Cover it with detail paper, and hold both papers down firmly. Use the blunt, unsharpened end of the pencil and, holding it absolutely vertical, rub it round and round in a circular motion, covering the whole area. The watermark design will then appear. It is difficult to make a very dark image of a watermark.

Graffiti

Graffiti are writings or scratchings on plaster, walls, wood and other surfaces.

It is easy to make and rub your own graffiti. Mix up some plaster of Paris and pour it into an old cardboard box to set. Tear off the cardboard and write or draw on the plaster block with a pointed nail or penknife. The surface texture will give an interesting background to your design. Now rub the design using paper and wax in the usual way.

Paintings

It is possible to make rubbings from your own paintings if you have applied the paint thickly.

Use emulsion or polymer paints, or mix powdered paint with a Medium such as Marvin or Gel. The Medium is water based and quick drying. It has adhesive properties and will stick to all kinds of paper, wood and card. You can sprinkle scraps of fabric, split peas, string, sand and so on onto the surface while it is still wet. This gives added interest to the texture of the picture. If you do your painting on card or hardboard you will have a good surface on which to rub when it is finished.

The effect you gain from this kind of rubbing is similar to that of taking a print of a painting while it is still wet. But the advantage of this method is in the number of prints that can be made.

Make sure you paint your picture with bold strong brush strokes. Allow the paint to dry perfectly before rubbing or you will simply flatten the paint.

Clean your brushes immediately after painting by stirring them in water and working the colours out in an old cloth. In the colour does dry on the brush, soak it in methylated spirit. Clearly, the longer the paint is left on the brush, the more difficult it will be to remove.

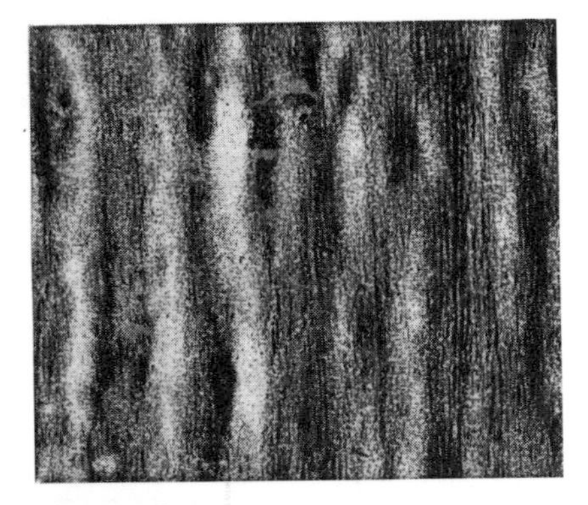
cucumber

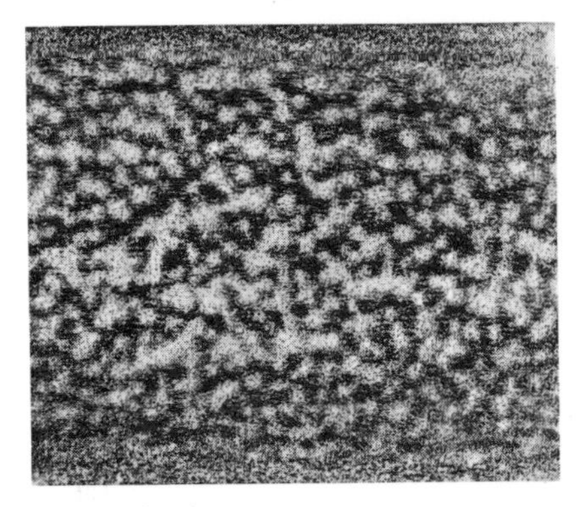
grapefruit

onion

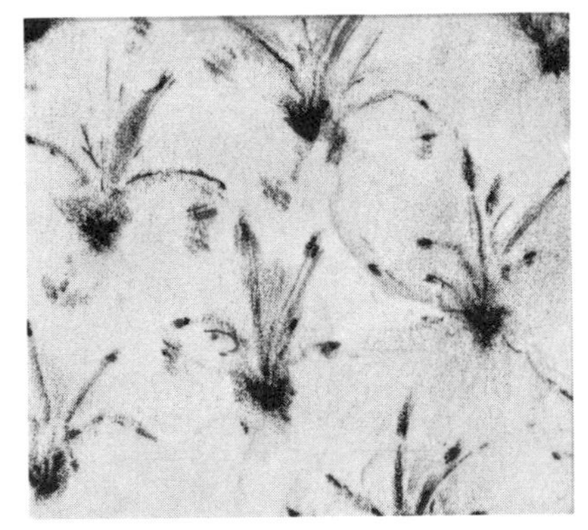
pineapple

parsnip

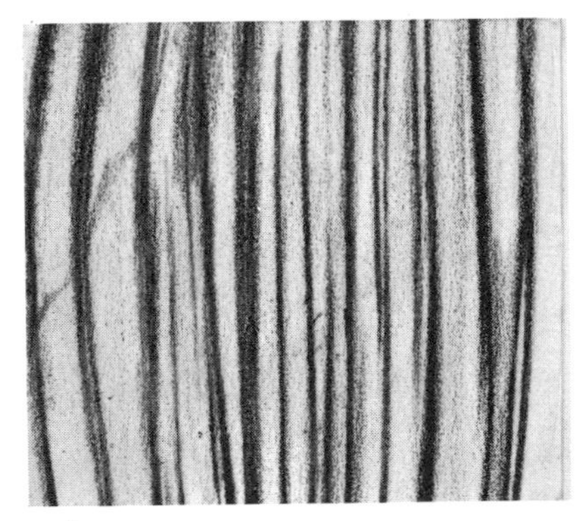
celery

Fruit and vegetables

Certain fruit and vegetables can make good rubbings. The surface textures themselves can give varied effects. Compare rubbings of a pineapple, an orange and a grapefruit.

It is also possible to make rubbings of the textures inside some fruit and vegetables. First cut them in half or into slices and leave them to dry. Cut them and leave them overnight or place them near direct heat which will help to seal the juices. Make sure you cut straight through the object so as to produce a flat surface for rubbings.

You can make rubbings from apples, pears, carrots, parsnips, cabbages and savoys, and many more. Naturally the very soft fruits are not suitable.

Tissue paper and soft wax crayons are usually best for this type of rubbing.

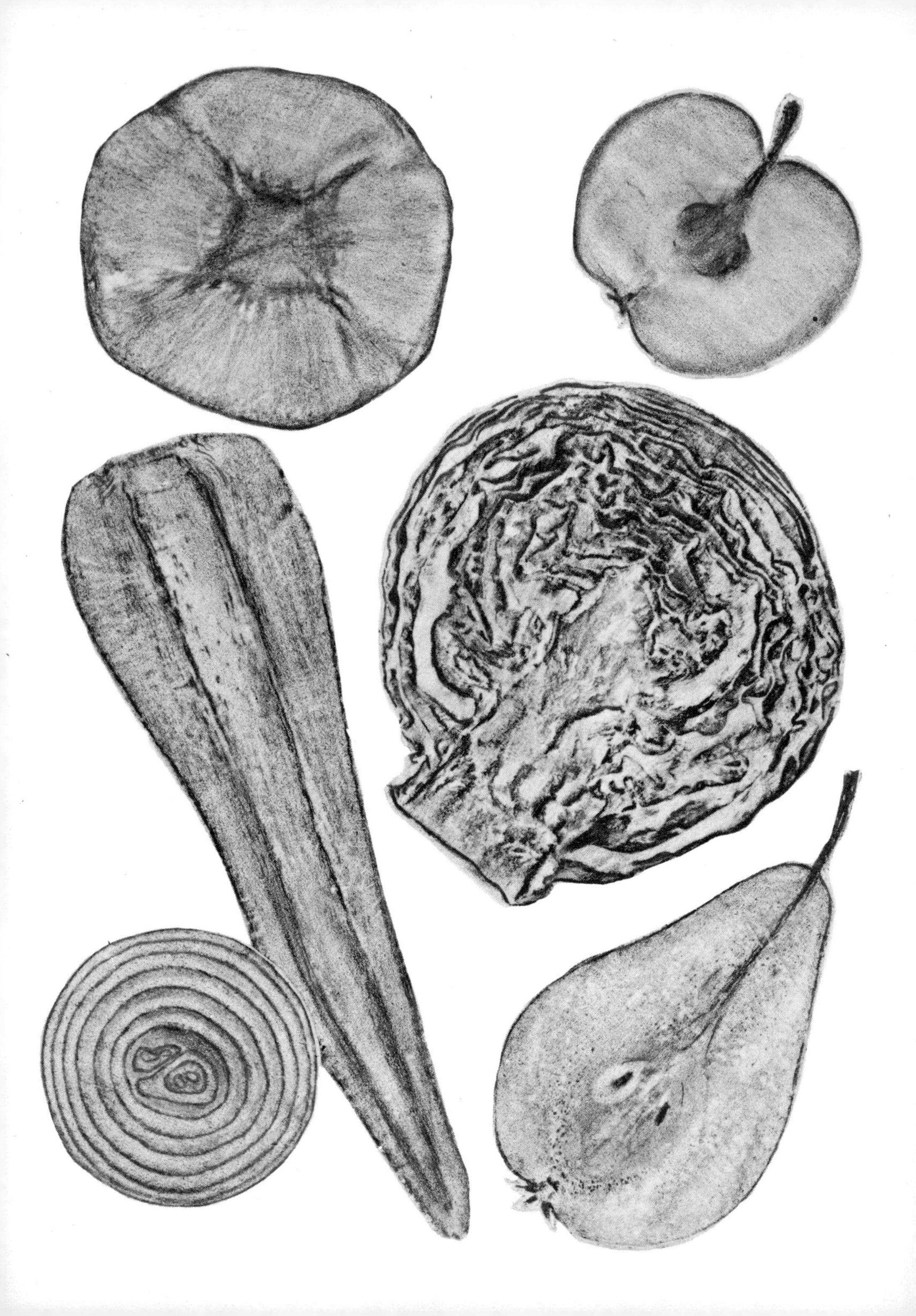

Manhole covers

See how many manhole covers you can spot as you walk along the street. Some of them will be very old. And once you have started looking you will be surprised how many different shapes and designs you can find, some of them very beautiful.

Make sure you clean any loose grit or dirt away from the surface with a brush before you start rubbing. Fix the paper with masking tape or hold it down with stones or weights.

Rubbings as interior decoration

Murals. Just one way of using your rubbings is to decorate a wall, possibly the wall of your own room. A design of manhole covers looks particularly effective on a white or plain-coloured wall.

Cut out your circles or shapes carefully. Paste each one to the wall with Polycell or a similar wallpaper paste.

If your designs were rubbed on white paper and you intend pasting them on a coloured wall, paste them onto thicker white paper or card before you cut them out. This will retain the whiteness and stop the wall colour showing through. In this case, use Cow gum or rubber cement to stick the designs to the wall.

GAMES

Cupboards. This cupboard door is decorated with sections of manhole covers arranged in a circle. Remember that these can be brightly coloured. Cut each section carefully and arrange the pieces on a flat surface, making sure that they fit exactly. Mark the centre of the door. Glue on one section at a time, making sure the point of each section touches the point in the centre of the door. If the cupboard is used a great deal you can cover the rubbings with transparent self-adhesive plastic.

Chest of drawers. The designs you choose could be in one or more colours, and could be the same or different on each drawer. Alternatively, you could rub the names of the items kept in each drawer – games, toys, clothes, for example – using the method described on page 26.

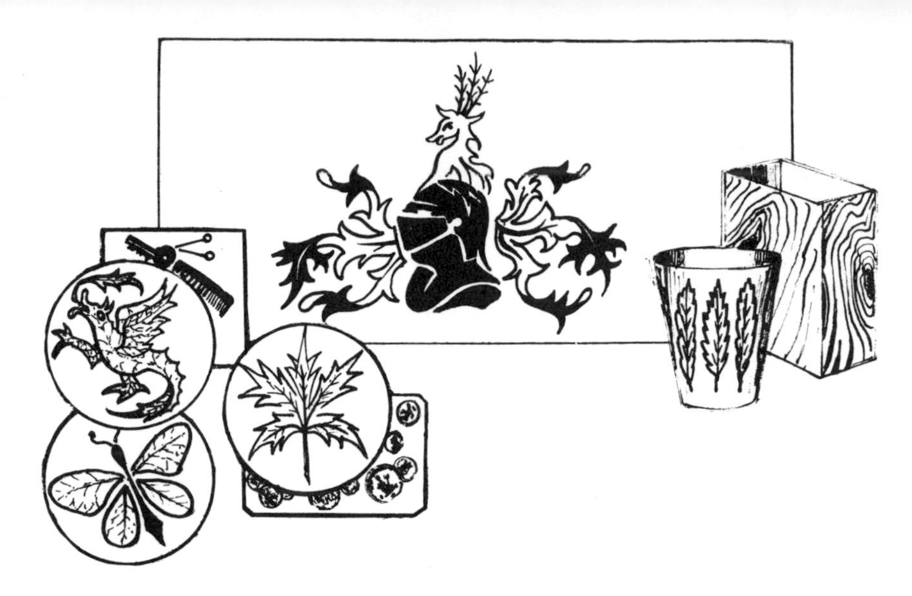

Table mats. Glue some of your designs onto pieces of wood or hardboard. Cover them with transparent self-adhesive plastic.

Bedheads. A coat of arms looks very impressive in red, gold or black. Cover the rubbing with self-adhesive plastic, cut it out carefully, and glue or paste it to the bedhead.

Waste paper bins. You can redecorate a bin you already have or find a tin or cardboard container that would be suitable. Simply choose some rubbings to fit your colour scheme, glue them on, and cover the bin with self-adhesive plastic.

Doors. A brass rubbing looks very attractive on a door. Cut the design out carefully and paste it straight onto the door. The paintwork will make a perfect mount or frame.

Many other kinds of rubbings would look good on doors too. Just cut them out and try them. You could also make special designs for each room or rub their names.

Making bookmarks

It is very simple indeed to make your rubbings into bookmarks.

Simply stick them onto strips of white or coloured card. When the glue has dried, cover them with clear, self-adhesive plastic.

You could also use leather or fabric instead of card. Fray the ends of the material or cut the leather into a fringe to make it more interesting.

Making Christmas cards

On the facing page are some ideas for decorating cards with your rubbings.

Designs can be made especially to suit your friends and relations by choosing objects to rub that you know they would like. Alternatively, you could draw designs on card and cut them out, or you could use animals, flowers, ships, names and numbers printed on chocolate boxes, old cards and the like. Paste them onto a piece of card and leave them to dry. Cover them with lining or architects' detail paper, and rub in the usual way with one or more coloured crayons. Mount the rubbing on thick paper, white or coloured card. If you have rubbed over the edge of the design by mistake, cut it out before you mount it.

Excellent rubbings may be reproduced from a lino-cut.

Since this method enables you to make several rubbings from the same design, you could make all your Christmas cards from the same original. So make sure you are perfectly satisfied with the design before you start to rub.

Keeping a scrapbook

Stick any rubbings you are not using into a scrapbook. This will keep them clean and flat and generally protect them.

Arrange them attractively in patterns. Group the same subjects together or mix them, just as you wish.

Paste the rubbings onto one side of the paper only, in case at some later date you should decide to remove some, possibly for use as decoration. This way you will avoid cutting others.

The cover of the book could be decorated with rubbings and finally covered with clear self-adhesive plastic.

Common faults

Blurred image. This is caused by letting the paper move slightly while you are rubbing. Always make sure the paper is taped down firmly. Take your time over the rubbing, covering only a small area at a time and working from the top of the design towards the bottom.

Paper tears. This may well be caused by using paper that is too thin. Remember to rub very lightly at first to reveal any sharp edges.

Smudging. This could be caused by using unsuitable materials. Astral heelball will always give good results. Buy a fixative to 'fix' soft crayon or pencil.

Wax resist. If the wax does not show through the paint it will probably mean that the paint is too thick. The wax must be applied thickly, and the paint must be thin.

Materials and suppliers

Rubbing equipment including Astral heelball and powdered graphite from:

Phillips and Page Ltd, 50 Kensington Church Street, London W8. Mail orders in U.K. and abroad.

Harvard Square Art Center, 1099 Massachusetts Avenue, Cambridge, Mass. 01238.

New York Central Supply Company, 62 Third Avenue, New York, N.Y. 10003

Oakes on the Hill, 10 Thomas Street, Providence, R.I. 02920

Metal foil, papers including tissue and detail; a wide variety of coloured wax crayons including non-smudge; Reeves Polymer colours and medium from:

Reeves and Sons Ltd, 13 Charing Cross Road, London WC2

Reeves and Sons (Canada) Ltd, 16 Apex Road, Toronto

Reeves and Sons (Canada) Ltd., 519 West Pender Street, Vancouver B.C.

Stafford-Reeves, Inc., 626 Greenwich Street, New York 10014

Index